Twilightofthefreakingods

a play by Stan's Cafe

ISBN 978-1-913185-23-7

Published by Stan's Cafe
Birmingham, UK
2020

www.stanscafe.co.uk

Twilightofthefreakingods © Stan's Cafe 2013
Photos © Graeme Braidwood 2013
Stills © Reel Access 2013
Publication © Stan's Cafe 2020

Contents:

Programme Notes	1
Map of the stage	5
Tips For Performing Twilightofthefreakingods	6
Brünnhilde	7
Gutrune	11
Machinist #1	14
Hagen	16
Gunther	20
Child	23
Machinist #2	24
Woglinde & Norn #1	26
Wellgunde & Norn #2	29
Alberich & Wotan	32
Waltraute	36
Flosshilde & Norn #3	39
Machinist #3	41
Costume Making	44
Siegfried	45
Instructions for the speaking clock	50
Making *Twilightofthefreakingods*	51

Edited Programme Note

Alberich & Wotan	Michael Radford
Brünnhilde	Chris Dugrenier
Child	Eve Yarker
Flosshilde & Norn #3	Rebecca Greenhalgh
Gunther	Jake Oldershaw
Gutrune	Amy Taylor
Hagen	Jack Trow
Machinist #1	Craig Stephens
Machinist #2	James Yarker
Machinist #3	Rochi Rampal
Siegfried	Graeme Rose
Waltraute	Olivia Winteringham
Wellgunde & Norn #2	Maria-Angela Wells
Woglinde & Norn #1	Katherine Lunney
Forklift Driver	John Stych
Sound	Nina West
Costume Sculpture	Denise Stanton
Costume	Kay Wilton
Props and Lots	Craig Stephens
Lighting	Jim Wyatt-Lees + Mick Diver
Photography	Graeme Braidwood
P.R.	Dave Freak
Video	Reel Access
Timetable	James Yarker
Office Assistant	Philip Holyman
General Manager	Charlotte Martin

Thanks to:
Michael Wolters for the Nietzsche. Chris Hall at Bacchus Bar. Philip Holyman, Lucy Nicholls & Harry Trow. The Stan's Cafe board of directors plus Nick Sweeting. John Sloyan and A E Harris & Co., mac birmingham, Theatre Ark and The REP. Dan Pursey at Mobius. Reel Access, Flatpack and the University of Stafford. The cast and crew for their trust and commitment.

Thank you for joining us in this theatrical experiment. The performance takes place across three rooms. You cannot physically see into all rooms simultaneously, so you will probably want to change your viewing position during the show. Please be careful when moving about the auditorium.

The show aspires to be a bit like test match cricket, absorbing, occasionally exciting but also a social occasion, not intended to be watched in total silence. The bar will remain open throughout the show and toasted sandwiches are on sale outside.

Twilightofthefreakingods is Wagner's *Götterdämmerung* without the music or libretto but with timings mapped from George Solti's recording of the opera. The show is unrehearsed and runs from a timetable with a separate list of instructions for each performer.

If you are unfamiliar with *Götterdämmerung* and feel your experience would be improved by knowing the plot a very rough précis is given here.

Prologue: The Rope of Destiny snaps. Siegfried gives Brünnhilde The Ring of Power and goes off down the Rhine seeking adventure.

Act 1 Scene 1: In the Hall of the Gibichungs, Hagen advises his half brother, Gunther, to marry Brünnhilde and his half sister Gutrune, to marry Siegfried.

Act 1 Scene 2: Siegfried is drugged so he falls in love with Gutrune and agrees to win Brünnhilde for Gunther.

Act 1 Scene 3: Brünnhilde is visited by her sister Waltraute, who reports that Wotan, their father, is in decline and has sent two ravens to spy on the world. She begs for the cursed ring to be returned to the Rhinemaidens, from who it was originally stolen. Brünnhilde keeps the ring, then Siegfried, in disguise, steels it.

Act 2 Scene 1: Hagen is visited by his father Alberich, who explains that with the ring they can have power over the whole world.

Act 2 Scene 2: Siegfried returns and tells the story of his adventure.

Act 2 Scene 3: Hagen tells everyone to get ready for a wedding party.

Act 2 Scene 4: Gunther arrives with Brünnhilde, who is astonished to see the ring on Siegfried's hand and to find he is to marry Gutrune. Brünnhilde accuses Siegfried of betraying her and he swears on a spear that this is untrue.

Act 2 Scene 5: Brünnhilde, Hagen and Gunther plot Siegfried's death.

Act 3 Scene 1: Out hunting Siegfried meets the Rhinemaidens, who try to persuade him to return the ring to them and remind him of its curse. He is unconcerned.

Act 3 Scene 2: Siegfried meets up with Gunther and Hagen and tells them of his youthful adventures. He is given a potion, which restores his memory of Brünnhilde. He is distracted by Wotan's ravens and is stabbed.

Act 3 Scene 3: Siegfried eventually dies. Gutrune is distraught and dies. Hagen kills Gunther in a struggle for the ring. The Rheinmaidens drown Hagen and Brünnhilde rides her horse into the flames of Siegfried's funeral pyre with the ring, which will be purged of its curse by the flames.

Twilightofthefreakingods is a celebration of five years of performances in our home venue, @ A E Harris. It is the final performance to take place in the venue's large format. In the New Year it will re-open as a fifty-seat venue. Stan's Cafe would like to thank our landlords, Arts Council England, friends, colleagues and audiences who have made it all possible. This is our second 'austerity' production, so Stan's Cafe devotees may enjoy trying to spot items from previous shows in this one.

I would personally like to thank Charlotte and Craig. This venue has been built on their incredible skills, commitment and goodwill. By extension I'd also like to thank their families (and mine) for being so ridiculously tolerant when hearing the phrase "I've just got to nip down to the space" or "yes, I'm just locking up now". You've made this special thing possible.

Let's celebrate… *Twilightofthefreakingods*.

James Yarker 10/10/13

Map of the Stage

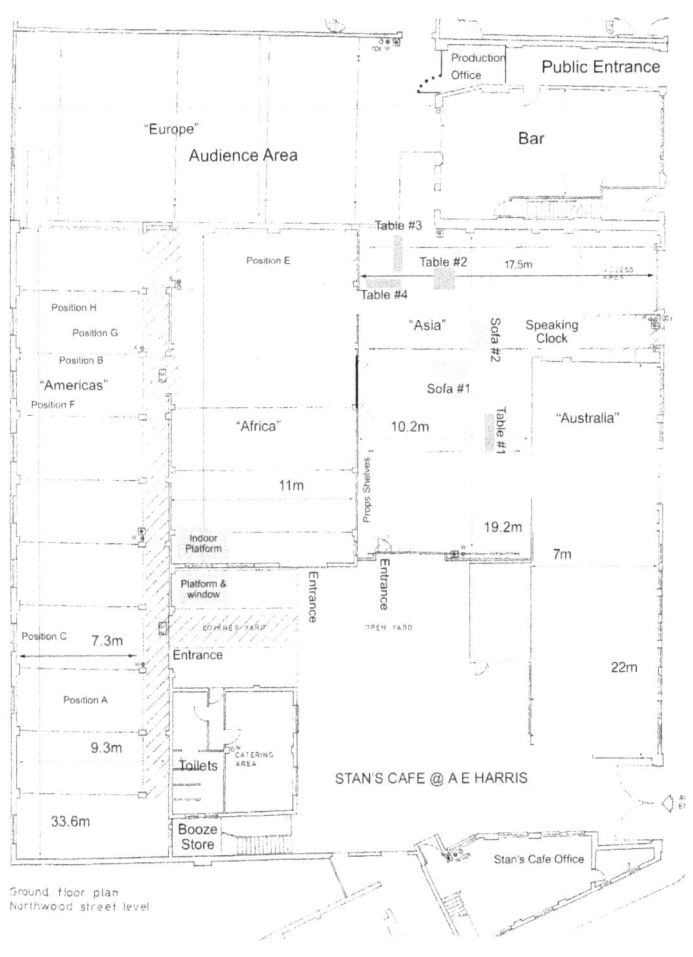

Tips for performing Twilightofthefreakingods.

Have confidence and commit to it.
Concentrate hard.
Try and memorise the timetable in sequences, check points you can revise when not in scenes.
If you get stuck improvise in the spirit of the show.
If you get very stuck put one hand up and someone with a timetable will come and rescue you.
Don't worry, some things are timetabled to arrive fast at the last minute.
You will have to move yourself around a bit in scenes to make them work as doing this by instruction is impossible!
Practice moving at the correct pace – work out the maths of certain moves.

Chris Dugrenier: Brünnhilde

20:00	Enter America from the courtyard in your base costume.
20:01	Turn right and approach your special costume
20:02	Put your arms into your costume (it will be put on you). Wait.
20:06	(Scene is played in reverse) wave goodbye to Siegfried as he arrives.
20:10	Kiss Siegfried farewell.
20:11	When Siegfried has looked at the bicycle for a few moments gesture to it and bring your arm back in and down to your side.
20:12	Look at your ring in delight. Siegfried will clasp your hands then take the ring off your finger. As he goes to put the ring in his pocket look amazed.
20:13	Embrace Siegfried and start to walk backwards with your arms extended for the embrace. After you have moved back your arms go to your sides.
20:14	Walk backwards.
20:15	Close to the back wall turn to face the windows and reverse into the Booze Store (once you are hidden pull the bottom of your dress in behind you).
20:16	Rest (find spare ring and put it on).
20:39	Reverse out of the Booze Store into America.
20:40	Halfway to the window turn and reverse towards the audience.
20:44	Pause hold your left hand up in the air so the audience can see it. Look at the ring.
20:56	Your costume should have left America into the Courtyard now.
21:04	Sneak into the back of Africa.
21:06	Sneak into the back of the orange mass.
21:09	Look majestic as the orange declines.
21:10	Try to embrace Waltraute.

21:11	Gesture ('What's going on? What's happening at home?').
21:12	Gesture ('I'm so pleased to see you. What's wrong?')
21:13	Look towards America.
21:14	Listen (worried).
21:18	Look towards America.
21:19	Hold your ring, listening.
21:21	Gesture ('It's the ring Siegfried gave me and I'm not letting go of it').
21:22	Let Waltraute take your hand.
21:23	Resist.
21:25	Banish Waltraute.
21:27	Neutral.
21:28	Disappear into flames.
21:31	('Who is this?')
21:32	('Who are you?')
21:33	Hold hand up with ring and point to it.
21:34	Point him away.
21:35	Look in horror as Siegfried reaches for your wrist.
21:36	Silent scream.
21:37	Silent agony.
21:38	Reach out for ring.
21:39	Beat chest.
21:40	Turn around and crouch down.
21:41	When the fabric has covered you exit into the courtyard.
21:43	Enter Asia from Australia.
21:44	Rest on Sofa #2.
21:53	Leave via Australia at America/Courtyard door get into the boat.
21:54	Look majestic.
22:12	Step off boat, helped by Gunther.
22:13	Look around mystified.
22:14	Start to tremble.
22:15	Point at Siegfried and Gutrune.
22:16	Point to yourself ('I am your wife').
22:17	Look at the ring and start to tremble again.
22:18	Trembling.

22:19	Point at the ring.
22:20	Pointing at the ring.
22:21	Look at everyone in the group.
22:22	Slowly point at Siegfried.
22:23	Look at Siegfried whilst pointing.
22:24	Take your finger down slowly.
22:25	Look at Siegfried.
22:26	Watch.
22:27	Grab spear.
22:28	Gesture at Siegfried ('Go away deceitful man').
22:29	Watch them go.
22:33	Watch them arrive.
22:37	Look at person with the spear (Hagen then Gunther).
22:38	Take spear from Gunther.
22:39	Look at person with the spear (Hagen).
22:40	Look at person with the spear (Gunther).
22:41	Take spear from Gunther.

22:42	Look at person with the spear (Hagen).
22:43	Look at person with the spear (Gunther).
22:44	Take spear from Gunther.

22:45	Look at person with the spear (Hagen).
22:46	Exit Africa into America. Move DS from the door.
22:50	When the bouncy castle arrives move backwards and sit on it.
23:03	Stand up from bouncy castle move around it and out of America into courtyard.
23:11	Be posed by the window on the outdoor platform looking magnificent.
23:12	Move in this pose.
23:13	Rest.
23:19	Be posed at the window again, looking in on the scene in Africa.
23:24	Move off platform and into Asia from Australia.
23:25	Take your elaborate costume off.
23:26	Go to Kay at Tables #4 & #5, put your new costume on. Have it fitted. When your costume is fitted start walking to Africa.
23:37	Enter Africa.
23:38	Approach Siegfried's body.
23:39	Kiss Siegfried's body.
23:40	Wave others away.
23:41	Sit with body.
23:45	Take ring from Siegfried's finger before sheet covers him.
23:46	Stand up.
23:47	Watch as the body is taken away.
23:50	Beckon your horse.
23:53	Climb on your horse and start peddling.
23:56	When doors close behind you stop peddling.
23:57	Stand in the courtyard facing the Asia doors.
00:01	Have a rest, have a beer and meet your fans.

Amy Taylor: Gutrune

19:55   Enter Asia from Australia and sit on the SR end of Sofa #1, blow up balloons so they surround you.

20:20   Stop blowing up balloons, make sure none are on the sofa. Be prepared to keep the sofa balanced.
20:24   Look at Hagen.
20:25   Listen and nod.
20:27   Look at Gunther.
20:28   Look at Hagen.
20:29   Gesture ('What about me?')
20:30   Look at Hagen.
20:31   Follow Hagen's gesture to look at Asia.
20:32   Smile at Hagen and nod.
20:33   Turn to look at door to America ('What's that?')
20:37   Stand as Seigfried approaches.
20:38   Gesture to Siegfried ('Welcome').
20:40   Listen to Siegfried.
20:42   Take cup from Gunther and give it to Siegfried.
20:43   Watch Siegfried.
20:45   Smile at Siegfried.

20:46	Hold your hand out to Siegfried.
20:47	Clasp your hands to your chest.
20:48	Watch the action.
20:53	Reach out to Siegfried your departing lover.
20:54	Turn away.
20:56	Hold your head in your hands.
20:57	Make yourself comfortable and stay still.
21:55	Hold your pose.
21:56	Watch Siegfried.
21:58	Move to Siegfried.
21:59	Have hand kissed.
22:00	Hold Siegfried's hand.
22:12	You are delighted to see Gunther again.
22:14	Point at Brünnhilde with concern.
22:15	Hold Siegfried's hand tighter ('Yes, we're married').
22:16	Shake your head whilst looking at Brünnhilde.
22:17	Look at Brünnhilde.
22:19	Look at the ring.

22:21	Look at Brünnhilde.
22:22	As Brünnhilde points at Siegfried look at him.
22:25	Look on with concern.

22:28	Take Siegfried's arm and turn, starting to walk towards Asia.
22:30	Enter Asia, put on wedding costume, drink beer, put on make-up.
22:32	Take Siegfried's right arm in your left arm and walk proudly into Africa along the white carpet.
22:37	Climb onto the bouncy castle. Try and have the ring put you your finger without any other contact. Try and kiss your husband without holding him. Then drink wine, eat sandwiches, sit in inflatable chairs.
22:46	Step off bouncy castle. Walk into America stand DS from main doorway facing the audience.
23:50	The bouncy castle should have arrived, without looking around walk backwards to sit on it.
23:03	Sleep on the bouncy castle.
23:20	Wake up and stand up. Start walking towards America.
23:30	Enter America.
23:31	Weep over Siegfried's body.
23:33	Push Gunther away and continue to weep over Siegfried's body.
23:37	Back slowly out of Africa.
23:45	Enter America. Run through America screaming and out into the courtyard.
23:57	Stand in Courtyard looking at door into Asia holding a flaming torch.
23:59	When the door to Asia is closed extinguish your torch.
00:01	Have a rest, have a beer and meet your fans.

Craig Stephens: Machinist #1

19:45	Open the America/Courtyard door for Eve. Light torch for James & hand it to him.
19:49	Enter Asia from courtyard carrying one spool.
19:50	Roll this spool and the two others into America.
19:52	Tie thread off to pillar US Africa – Asia door 1.5 m from ground and to Table #2.
19:53	Stand and watch
19:56	End of standing and watching.
20:06	Stand by ring.
20:12	Lift ring down.
20:13	Ring into Asia and placed over Table #2 and anyone there.
20:14	Exit Asia.
20:15	Into Booze Store in America.
20:16	Pull Rhine into first position by taking the SR end and pulling out DSR corner.
20:17	Exit.
20:18	Slide pallet truck under Sofa #1.
20:19	Pull Sofa #1 towards Africa.
20:21	Pallet truck into Africa.
20:23	Set performers SR of centre.
20:24	Park pallet truck at the back of the space.
20:36	Help Machinist #3 pull Rhine into position by placing a table in the appropriate place in the centre of the Africa/America door.
20:37	Pick Sofa #1 up from Africa with pallet truck.
20:38	Return Sofa #1 to Asia.
20:41	Pour drink on the floor in America position A.
20:57	Tie Waltraute to her chair with her apron strings.
20:59	Set up flowers DSR in America.
21:00	Set up Red Rad (heater) on flowers.
21:01	Get into position DSL in Africa.
21:03	Run in with fabric over Gutrune and Wellgrunde. Exit

	Africa/Courtyard door.
21:04	Open fire doors for Brünnhilde.
21:05	Get orange mass into position and turn fan on.
21:09	Fan off.
21:26	Fan on.
21:30	Fan off.
21:39	Fan on.
21:41	Fan off and orange mass into Courtyard.
22:00	In courtyard gather cloth in from Albreich.
22:01	Into Asia from Courtyard. When Albreich is in turn bouncy castle on.
22:32	Unroll dining roll on floor from Asia to America.
22:46	Spill water into America from Courtyard and start mopping the floor.

22:52   Stop mopping.

23:09   Move to the Speaking Clock
23:10 – 23:29   You are the Speaking Clock.

23:36	Give a sword to Gunther.
23:47	Move Siegfried out of Africa with pallet truck.
23:48	Set Siegfried on pallet central in Asia for the fork lift.
23:52	Take down blackout over Africa/Courtyard exit. Brünnhilde climbs on the horse.
23:53	Operate fans and open door to the Courtyard.
23:56	Close Courtyard doors, drag out globe and start inflating it. Try to lift and carry globe, fail to squeeze it into America, throw yourself against it.
00:00	Stop in blackout.
00:01	Have a rest, have a beer and meet your fans.

Jack Trow: Hagen

19:56	Enter Asia from Australia and sit on the SR end of Sofa #1, blow up balloons so they surround you.
20:04	Walk to the speaking clock
20:05 – 20:22	You are the speaking clock.
20:23	Walk into Africa.
20:24	Stand stage left of Sofa #1.
20:25	Gesture to Gunther and Gutrune.
20:27	Gesture to America.
20:29	Neutral.
20:30	Gesture to Asia.
20:32	Gesture to Gutrune.
20:33	Turn to look at door to America ('What's that?').
20:37	Gesture to Siegfried ('Welcome').
20:40	Listen to Siegfried.
20:41	You are given potion, pour a few drops into the goblet.
20:42	Watch the action and hold potion out to be taken away from you.
20:43	Watch Siegfried.
20:45	Keep watching Siegfried, put your hand out behind you for the sword.

20:47	When you have the sword hold it out to Gunther's hand.
20:48	Cut the palm of Gunther's hand.
20:49	Hold sword out and cut the palm of Siegfried's hand.
20:50	Watch & fix sword in belt.
20:51	Clasp the shaking hands together.
20:52	Let go of hands.
20:53	Watch.
20:54	Wave.
20:58	Light candle. Take sword out of belt and walk backwards towards Indoor Platform.
20:59	Place candle on edge of Platform (position marked), climb to sit there.
21:00	Gesture around (summarising the story as you see it from your perspective).
21:04	You are on lookout, but mostly focus on trying to complete the Rubic's Cube waiting for you on the platform. Try and keep the cube held in camera shot beside the light.
21:46	When you hear knocking at window, turn to it and put Rubic's Cube down.
21:47	Stand up on the platform and move to the window.
21:48	Look from the small globe outside to the big globe inside.
21:49	Gesture ('How are we to do that?').
21:50	Watch.
21:51	Gesture ('Gunther's gone with Siegfried now').
21:52	Watch then turn.
21:53	Move to the DSR corner of the platform looking at the globe.
21:54	Look back at the window.
21:55	Climb down from the platform and blow out the candle.
21:56	Watch Siegfried and Gutrune.
22:01	Move towards Asia door calling Vassells to prepare a party.
22:04	At door indicate the important guests who are waiting.
22:06	Stand back and watch contented as the Vassells

	come in.
22:10	You are delighted when Gunther and Brünnhilde arrive.
22:11	Exit Africa go and rest on Sofa #2.
22:18	Pick up spear from props shelves start carrying it towards Africa.
22:21	Enter Africa with the spear. Move towards the central group.
22:23	Bring the spear slowly up into the centre of the group.
22:26	Hold the spear still.
22:27	Watch as the spear is grabbed etc..
22:29	Watch Siegfried and Gutrune go off.
22:33	Watch Siegfried and Gutrune arrive.
22:37	Gunther takes the spear from you, you look at him.
22:38	When Brünnhilde takes the spear look at her.
22:39	Take the spear from Brünnhilde.
22:40	Gunther takes the spear from you, you look at him.
22:41	When Brünnhilde takes the spear look at her.
22:42	Take the spear from Brünnhilde.
22:43	Gunther takes the spear from you, you look at him.
22:44	When Brünnhilde takes the spear look at her.
22:45	Take the spear from Brünnhilde.
22:46	Exit Africa to America. Stand DS of door facing the audience.
22:50	When the bouncy castle is in place walk backwards and sit on it.
23:03	Walk into Africa.
23:04	Embrace Siegfried.
23:05	Listen to his story.
23:07	Big laughs.
23:09	You are given a goblet. Offer Siegfried the goblet.
23:10	Watch Siegfried.
23:14	Move to stab Siegfried.
23:15	Stab Siegfried.

23:16	Watch Siegfried.
23:24	Turn to America.
23:30	Watch Gutrune as she arrives.
23:32	Move to comfort Gutrune.
23:34	Gunther blames you for the murder. Shake your head.
23:35	Blame Gunther for the murder.
23:36	Approach the body to take the ring.
23:37	You are given a sword. Have a sword fight with Gunther and stab him.
23:38	Watch Gunther dying. You are grabbed and walked to the bouncy castle.
23:41	Climb on the bouncy castle and try to maintain a dignified pose as it deflates.
23:43	Try repeatedly to 'swim to the surface' as the bouncy castle deflates.
22:44	You are bundled out of America wrapped in a bouncy castle.
23:57	Stand in courtyard facing Asia door.
23:58	Stand in courtyard facing Asia door.
00:01	Have a rest, have a beer and meet your fans.

Jake Oldershaw: Gunther

19:54	Enter Asia from Australia and sit on the SL end of Sofa #1, blow up balloons so they surround you.
20:20	Stop blowing up balloons, make sure none are on sofa. Be prepared to keep the sofa balanced.
20:24	Look at Hagen.
20:25	Gesture to Hagen ('You are tremendous').
20:27	Gesture to yourself ('What about me?').
20:28	Look at Gutrune.
20:30	Look at Hagen.
20:31	Follow Hagen's gesture to look at Asia.
20:32	Smile at Hagen and nod.
20:33	Turn to look at door to America ('What's that?').
20:37	Stand as Siegfried approaches.
20:38	Gesture to Siegfried ('Welcome').
20:40	Listen to Siegfried.
20:41	Be given Goblet, then hold it out to Hagen.
20:42	Pass goblet to Gutrune.
20:43	Watch Siegfried.
20:47	When Siegfried turns to you, hold your hand out to Hagen.
20:48	Have your hand cut.
20:49	Hold your hand out to Siegfried.
20:51	Shake hands.
20:52	Let go of hand.
20:53	Get into boat.
20:54	Wave goodbye.
20:57	When boat is in Asia climb out.
20:58	Rest on Sofa #1.
21:20	Move to the Speaking Clock.
21:21 – 21:52	You are the Speaking Clock.
21:53	Exit Asia into Australia, go to Courtyard/America Entrance get in boat.
21:54	Row the boat.

22:10	Hands up (glorious return).
21:12	Step off boat when it stops in Africa.
21:13	Proudly introduce Brünnhilde.
21:14	Look concerned when Brünnhilde trembles.
22:16	Shake your head.
22:17	Look at Brünnhilde.
22:19	Look at the ring.
22:21	Look at Brünnhilde.
22:22	As Brünnhilde points at Siegfried look at him.
22:25	Look at spear.
22:26	Swear on spear.
22:27	Watch.
22:29	Watch them go.
22:33	Watch them arrive.
22:37	Take spear from Hagen.
22:38	Have spear taken from you by Brünnhilde, look at her.
22:39	When Hagen takes the spear look at him.
22:40	Take spear from Hagen.
22:41	Have spear taken from you by Brünnhilde, look at her.
22:42	When Hagen takes the spear look at him.
22:43	Take spear from Hagen.

22:44	Have spear taken from you by Brünnhilde, look at her.
22:45	When Hagen takes the spear, look at him.
22:46	Exit Africa into America. Stand DS of doorway facing audience.
22:50	When bouncy castle is in place walk backwards and sit on it.
23:03	Stand up and go into Africa.
23:04	Embrace Siegfried.
23:05	Listen to his story.
23:07	Big laughs.
23:09	Watch.
23:10	Watch Siegfried.
23:14	Watch Hagen.
23:15	Gasp as Siegfried is stabbed.
23:19	Watch as Siegfried sits up.
23:24	Turn to America.
23:30	Watch Gutrune as she arrives.
23:32	Move to comfort Gutrune.
23:34	When you are pushed away blame Hagen.
23:35	He blames you – shake your head.
23:36	You are given a sword, fight Hagen as he tries to get ring from Siegfried.
23:37	You fight and are stabbed.
23:38	Crawl on your belly towards Europe you will be given blood to bleed and leave a trail.
23:40	Enter Asia on your belly.
23:46	Enter Australia on your belly.
23:57	Stand in courtyard facing Asia door.
23:58	Stand in courtyard facing Asia door.
00:01	Have a rest, have a beer and meet your fans.

Eve Yarker: Child

19:45   Cycle America – Asia casually with hair tied back.

19:45   Repeat fast, frightened looking behind, hair untied.

James Yarker: Machinist #2

19:45	After Eve, use her bike, cycle slowly America – Asia with lit torch .
20:11	Reverse into America from Courtyard with stationary bike on pallet truck Position A.
20:15	Take pallet truck off to America door.
20:16	Take ring from Siegfried (off stage).
20:17	Start to pull pallet truck.
20:36	Pallet truck into Africa.

20:39	Siegfried Steps off.
20:40	Pallet truck into Asia.
20:41	Give goblet to Gunther.
20:51	Get boat in America.
20:52	Push boat into Asia.
20:53	Hold boat stable.
20:54	Push boat to Asia.
20:57	Enter Asia.
21:04	Help wheel Wotan into America, then leave it to Machinist #3.
21:37	Lift big ring off Table #2.
21:38	Hold it upright.

21:42	Bring ring to Africa.
21:43	Into Africa.
21:44	Hook up in Position E.
21:54	Push boat from America/Courtyard door.
22:10	Into Africa.
22:11	Pause for passengers to step off.
22:13	Boat into Asia.
22:33	Push bouncy castle into Central Africa as fast as you can.
22:43	Get bouncy castle into Position B in America as fast as you can.
22:52	Turn bubble machine on.
22:53	OHP water effect.
23:02	Stop water effect.
23:20	Put throne into position US America.
00:01	Have a rest, have a beer and meet your fans.

Katherine Lunney: Woglinde & Norn #1

19:14	Before the doors open you are set DS in America.
19:48	Stand up.
19:50	Move to Position B and face Africa.
19:51	Catch the first spool that comes towards you (go and get it if it doesn't make it to you).
19:52	With your two partners plait the thread trying to start the plait as far into Africa as possible.
20:00	Move the cord to the US edge of the door into Africa and hold it there.
20:03	When cord snaps put spool on floor and walk backwards horrified until you are by windows then spin to the left and crouch with your hands over your head. Hold this pose.
20:08	Turn and look out of the window.
20:16	Take your Norn blanket off and put on your Rhinemaiden headdress on.
20:17	Go to Position F.
20:18	With your hands out to the sides horizontally palms as vertical as possible turn clockwise or anti-clockwise at a pace you feel you can sustain without getting dizzy.

20:36	Stop spinning.
20:37	Exit America into the Courtyard.
20:39	Enter Asia from Australia. Go to Table #2, take the ring hold it up and look through it until the screaming stops.
20:40	Take off the blindfold and return it to the props shelf.
20:41	Move towards the Speaking Clock.
20:42 – 20:58	You are the Speaking Clock
20:59	Exit Asia into the Courtyard picking up a box of chalk and a kneeler from the props shelf on the way.
21:00	Starting in USR corner of America using the chalk write the story of the Götterdämmerung in letters 12" high. You can use the crib sheet provided, but try not to let the audience see it. Use a different colour for Acts and Scenes.

22:50	Conclude the text with "Act 3 Scene 1. Siegfried is out hunting. He stops by the river. Enter Rhinemaiden…" then you enter Africa from the DS America door. Join other Rhinemaiden by the ring.
22:51	Flirt with Siegfried.
22:56	Try and persuade Siegfried to give you the ring.

23:00	Warn him he will regret not giving you the ring. Follow blue fabric towards America.
23:03	Enter America.
23:04	Start pulling the bouncy castle US very slowly (take SL side).
23:20	The bouncy castle arrives at Point A. Rest out of sight.
23:30	Set off walking through America to Africa.
23:37	Enter Africa.
23:38	Grab Hagen and drag him to the bouncy castle and push him on it then loiter by the windows watching him.
23:41	As the bouncy castle collapses Hagen will try and keep his head clear of the collapsing material. Occasionally with the other Rhinemaiden fold the castle in on itself so Hagen cannot be seen for a bit.
23:44	With Hagen still in it help push the bouncy castle into the Courtyard.
23:57	Stand in the Courtyard looking at door into Asia holding a flaming torch.
23:59	When the door to Asia is closed extinguish your torch.
00:01	Have a rest, have a beer and meet your fans.

Maria Wells: Wellgunde & Norn #2

19:14	Before the doors open you are set DS in America.
19:48	Stand up.
19:50	Move to Position B and face Africa.
19:51	Catch the second spool that comes towards you (go and get it if it doesn't make it to you).

19:52	With your two partners plait the thread trying to start the plait as far into Africa as possible.
20:00	Move the cord to the US edge of the door into Africa and hold it there.
20:03	When cord snaps put spool on floor and walk backwards horrified until you are by windows then spin to the right and put your hands in the air. Hold this pose.
20:08	Turn and look out of the window.
20:16	Take your Norn blanket off and put on your Rhinemaiden headdress on.
20:17	Go to position G.
20:18	With your hands out to the sides horizontally palms as vertical as possible turn clockwise or anti-clockwise at a pace you feel you can sustain without

	getting dizzy.
20:36	Stop spinning.
20:37	Exit America into the Courtyard.
20:40	Enter Asia from Australia, go to the props shelf take off your headdress and put it on a shelf, then pick up the potion bottle.
20:41	Hand potion to Hagen who has his hand out for it, then wait.
20:42	Take potion off Hagen.
20:43	Return potion to the props shelf.
20:44	Take the sword from the props shelf and start travelling to Hagen with it.
20:47	Give sword to Hagen.
20:48	Watch the action from a step or two back, reacting subtly to what you see.
20:56	Move to comfort Gutrune.
20:57	Comfort Gutrune.
21:04	You will be covered by fabric. Make yourself as comfortable as possible but move as little as possible.
21:54	Watch action and react.
22:01	When Hagen calls Vassals to make merry, exit into Asia and load the bouncy castle with as many balloons as you can.
22:03	Make sandwiches at Table #1.
22:05	Make each other look as smart as possible.
22:06	Enter Africa and start a Welcome Choreography with your colleagues for whoever is about to enter Africa from America.
22:09	Hold frozen tableaux.
22:12	Frame the drama for the audience, occasionally change your position.
22:27	Back away from the action into Asia and start putting on party make up.
22:30	Drink beer.
22:32	Drink beer and put on party hat, pick up the tray of wine glasses.
22:33	Follow Siegfried and Brünnhilde into the centre of Africa along the white dining roll as part of the

	wedding parade.
22:37	Climb onto the bouncy castle and have a party. Hold tray whilst wine is ported into glasses. Eat sandwiches and dance.
22:46	Step off the bouncy castle and walk to SR of Position E where the ring is, hold your hands out in front of you ready for your headdress to arrive, when it does put it on.
22:51	Flirt with Siegfried.
22:56	Try and persuade Siegfried to give you the ring.
23:00	Warn him he will regret not giving you the ring, follow blue fabric towards America.
23:03	Enter America.
23:04	Start carrying fan US in America as the bouncy castle is dragged along, gather the power cable as you go so it does not go under the castle.
23:20	The Bouncy Castle arrives at Position A. Put the fan down and rest hidden from audience.
23:30	Set off walking through America to Africa.
23:37	Enter Africa.
23:38	Grab Hagen and drag him to the bouncy castle and push him on it then loiter around the plug socket.
23:41	Ostentatiously switch the plug off and pull it out of its socket. Hold the plug in the air. As the bouncy castle collapses Hagen will try and keep his head clear of the collapsing material. Occasionally fold the castle in on itself so Hagen cannot be seen for a bit.
23:44	With Hagen still in it, help push the bouncy castle into the Courtyard.
23:57	Stand in Courtyard looking at door into Asia holding a flaming torch.
23:59	When the door to Asia is closed extinguish your torch.
00:01	Have a rest, have a beer and meet your fans.

Michael Radford: Alberich & Wotan

19:45	Enter Asia from Australia. You are the Speaking Clock.
20:05	Sit at Table #2
20:12	Get the ring out of your pocket hold it up in front of your face and look through it.
20:15	Spin the ring repeatedly on the table seeing how long you can get it to spin for.
20:20	Continue your task despite being blindfolded. If the ring falls on the floor feel around until you find it, return to the table and continue.

20:34	Put the ring in your mouth.
20:36	Put your tongue out as far as you can with the ring on it.
20:39	When the ring is lifted off your tongue scream for a single breath.
20:40	Look directly ahead.
20:41	Pick up a cup and hold it out to your right. Look to your right.
20:42	Look in the cup, see there is nothing in there. Go to

	Table #1 for refreshment. Then sit on Sofa #2, blow up some balloons and rest.
21:02	Exit into courtyard and change into Wotan costume in kitchen.
21:03	Climb onto your throne by the America Courtyard door.
21:04	Whilst sitting look around you, be a bit lost. When you are at the window look out of it (still seated).

21:18	Gesture for two rooks to fly off around the world spying for you, then return to your previous pose.
21:36	Look round at America - Africa door.
21:37	Return to looking out of the window.
21:43	When you are out of America get off your throne and in Kitchen change into Albrich Costume.
21:46	Climb onto the outdoor platform and tap on the glass to attract Hagen's attention, beckon him to the window.
21:47	Gesture ('It's me, your father, don't you love me?').
21:48	Turn on the light in the globe and pick it up. Gesture ('You and I could have all this').
21:49	Watch response.
21:50	Gesture – with globe in hand (you need the ring).

21:51	Watch response.
21:52	Put globe down and move to SR window placing hands against the pane.
21:53	Move hands down to the lower half of the pane and push, so it opens. Climb in through the window.
21:54	Move to the DSL corner of the white fabric, stand off it, turn around, pick it up pull it around your shoulders as if it is a cape, walk into America dragging the fabric with you.
21:55	Keep walking diagonally into America to get as much of the fabric out of Africa as you can, then double round to walk US in America.
22:00	Exit America with fabric. Change to neutral costume and enter Asia through Australia.
22:01	Load bouncy castle with as many balloons as you can.
22:03	Make sandwiches at Table #1.
22:05	Make each other look as smart as possible.
22:06	Enter Africa and start Welcome Choreography with your colleagues for whoever is about to enter Africa from America.
22:09	Hold frozen tableaux.
22:12	Frame the drama for the audience, occasionally change your position.
22:29	Back away from the action into Asia.
22:30	Drink beer.
22:32	Drink beer and put on party hat, pick up sandwiches.
22:33	Follow Siegfried and Brünnhilde into the centre of Africa along the white dining roll as part of the wedding parade.
22:37	Climb onto the bouncy castle and have a party, share around and eat sandwiches.
22:46	Step off the bouncy castle and exit into Asia. Rest on Sofa #2 and clear up.

22:50 – 23:09 You are the Speaking Clock.

23:10	Take one of the umbrellas and shadow the actions of the other umbrella carrier (the umbrella is a raven).
23:12	With umbrella into Africa still shadowing other umbrella.
23:19	Into America with umbrella, still shadowing other umbrella. Fly umbrellas to behind the bouncy castle (you can be more freestyle now).
23:31	Sit on upturned throne behind the Bouncy Castle and rest.
23:44	Before you are revealed pick up your umbrella as if it is raining. Watch the action you see (not bouncy castle disappearing).
23:47	Stand up and start to walk to exit into the Courtyard.
23:50	Exit into Courtyard.
23:57	Stand in Courtyard looking at door into Asia holding a flaming torch.

23:59	When the door to Asia is closed extinguish your torch.
00:01	Have a rest, have a beer and meet your fans.

Olivia Winteringham: Waltraute

19:53	Enter from America/Courtyard door. Place mannequin at Position A then exit back into courtyard.
19:56	Dress mannequin in Brünnhilde's costume then stand beside lights SR.
20:02	Dress Brünnhilde then pick up mannequin and exit into courtyard.
20:04	Place mannequin US of Table #4 for Kay.
20:22	Find blindfold from the props shelf and blindfold the performer at Table #2. Move to the Speaking Clock.
20:23 – 20:41	You are the speaking clock.
20:57	Put your costume apron on and have it tied to a chair beside Australia door.
21:06	Pass into Africa.
21:07	Approach orange fabric.

21:10	Get close to Brünnhilde. As she tries to embrace you push her/yourself away. Walk backwards and sit on the chair you have been dragging.
21:11	Listen to Brünnhilde.
21:13	Gesture to America.
21:14	Gesture ('It's all going very badly').
21:15	Gesture ('Wotan is restless').
21:16	Gesture ('Now he is depressed').
21:17	Gesture ('And we sit around not doing anything').
21:18	Gesture ('He has sent ravens to spy on the world').
21:19	Gesture to Brünnhilde's ring ('We need that ring').
21:20	Gesture ('All our troubles are because of the ring, throw it in the Rhine').
21:21	Throw yourself on the floor and beg for the ring.
21:23	Try and get the ring by force.
21:25	Back away without the ring.
21:27	Exit Africa into America walking to Wotan in Position C.
21:32	Sit with Wotan looking out at the city.
21:36	Look round at Africa.
21:37	Look back at the city.
21:42	Pick up your chair and leave.
21:43	Via Australia go and rest on Sofa #2. Taking off your apron en route.
22:01	Load bouncy castle with balloons.
22:03	Quickly make sandwiches at Table #1.
22:05	Quickly put on make up.
22:06	Perform a Welcome Choreography in Africa for people who will eventually come in from America.
22:09	Hold a welcome tableaux.
22:12	Frame the action.
22:29	Exit into Asia.
23:30	Drink beer and open bubbly (don't pour it yet).
23:32	Continue to drink beer. Put on party hats.
22:33	Process in Africa behind Gutrune and Siegfried as if to wedding, carrying bubbly.
22:37	Climb onto the bouncy castle and have a party, try and pour bubbly into glasses. Eat sandwiches and dance.

22:49	Get an umbrella from the props shelves and fly it, in a big arc towards Africa.
23:12	Enter Africa with umbrella flying, circle the room.
23:19	Exit Africa into America. Fly the bird US.
23:32	Disappear behind the bouncy castle.
23:33	Put your apron on. Rest behind the bouncy castle.
23:44	When you are revealed be standing with your umbrella to protect you from rain. Have your left hand on Wotan's right shoulder. Your chair is attached to you by your apron. Look directly ahead rather than watch the bouncy castle go. Observe Gutrune running out.
23:47	Walk to exit into courtyard.
23:50	Exit.
23:57	Stand in the courtyard facing the Asia doors.
23:58	Keep standing until the big door is closed.
00:01	Have a rest, have a beer and meet your fans.

Rebecca Greenhalgh: Flosshilde & Norn #3

19:14	Before the doors open you are set DS in America.
19:48	Stand up.
19:50	Move to Position B and face Africa.
19:51	Catch the third spool that comes towards you (go and get it if it doesn't make it to you).
19:52	With your two partners plait the thread trying to start the plait as far into Africa as possible.
20:00	Move the cord to the US edge of the door into Africa and hold it there.
20:03	When cord snaps put spool on floor and walk backwards horrified until you are by windows then put your head back and both arms raise vertically toward the ceiling. Hold this pose.
20:08	Turn and look out of the window.
20:16	Take your Norn blanket off and put on your Rhine Maiden Headdress on.
20:17	Go to Position H.
20:18	With your hands out to the sides horizontally, palms as vertical as possible, turn clockwise or anti-clockwise at a pace you feel you can sustain without getting dizzy.
20:36	Stop spinning.
20:37	Exit America into the Courtyard.
20:38	Enter Asia from Australia, sit on Sofa #2 and blow up balloons.
20:58	Stop blowing up balloons.
20:59	Sit at Table #2 with both hands 8" above the tabletop palms down and fingers spread. When the typewriter arrives start typing. Type the story of Götterdämmerung.
22:45	Stop typing and sit back.
22:46	Watch what happens in front of you.
22:47	Move to Africa.
22:50	Arrive in Position E beside the other Rhine Maiden.
22:51	Flirt with Siegfried.
22:56	Try and persuade Siegfried to give you the ring.

23:00	Warn him he will regret not giving you the ring. Follow blue fabric towards America.
23:03	Enter America.
23:04	Start pulling the bouncy castle US very slowly (take SR side).
23:20	The bouncy Castle arrives at point A. Rest out of sight.
23:30	Set off walking through America to Africa.
23:37	Enter Africa.
23:38	Grab Hagen and drag him to the bouncy castle and push him on it then loiter by the windows watching him.
23:41	As the bouncy castle collapses Hagen will try and keep his head clear of the collapsing material. Occasionally with the other Rhinemaiden fold the castle in on itself so Hagen cannot be seen for a bit.
23:44	With Hagen still in it help push the bouncy castle into the Courtyard.
23:57	Stand in the Courtyard looking at door into Asia holding a flaming torch.
23:59	When the door to Asia is closed extinguish your torch.
00:01	Have a rest, have a beer and meet your fans.

Rochi Rampal: Machinist #3

19:45	Open the Asia/Courtyard Door 1m for Eve. Close the door after James as returned to courtyard with flaming torch.
19:49	Walk with two spools into Asia from Courtyard.
19:50	Hand spools to Machinist #1 when he needs them.
19:52	Tie thread off to pillar DS Africa – Asia door 1.5 m from ground.
19:53	Exit through Asia/Courtyard Door picking up knife from props self.
19:58	Enter Africa/Courtyard Door and start walking towards the ring.
20:01	Put arm and knife through the ring.
20:02	Hook knife under the cord.
20:03	Use other hand to push cord onto blade and cut it.
20:05	Withdraw knife from the ring and stand just SR of the ring.
20:12	Lift the ring (you will have help).
20:13	Place the ring over Table #2 and anyone sat at it. Stand and watch.
20:14	Exit Asia/Courtyard Door.
20:15	Enter America Courtyard Door and go into Booze Store.
20:16	Pull Rhine out of booze store. Take your corner to the SL side and stretch it out so the DS edge is by Position B. Stand and watch. Help if fabric gets badly caught in wheels.
20:36	Pull the front edge of the Rhine toward Africa.
20:41	Enter Africa.
20:45	Enter Asia.
20:57	The Rhine clears Africa. Pull it into a pile close to the Asia fire exit.
21:00	Take the typewriter from the props shelves and position in on Table #2.
21:01	Get into position DSR in Africa.
21:03	Run in with fabric over Gutrune and Wellgrunde. Exit Africa/Courtyard door.

21:04	Wheel Wotan on throne into America.
21:09	Wotan in place in Position C (path can meander).
21:10	Leaf drop on Wotan.
21:18	Pick up two black umbrellas from the trolley, open them and hold them up. Fly these two birds towards Africa.
21:31	Enter Africa and start to fly across the room.

21:37	Enter Asia.
21:40	Umbrellas on the props shelf.
21:41	Rest on Chair #1.
21:52	Approach the Speaking Clock.
21:53 – 22:51	You are the Speaking Clock (whilst on duty you have actions to fit in between announcements).
22:46	Set fire to the typing at Table #2.
22:47	Extinguish flames.
22:48	Take headdress to Wellgunde in Africa.
22:51	Last Speaking Clock announcement.
22:52	Turn on the bubble machine in Africa.
22:53	Pull Rhine through the ring in Africa into America (DSL door).
23:03	All the fabric is out of Africa.
23:47	Start moving horse to Brünnhilde
23:53	Brünnhilde climbs on the horse.
23:51	Push Brünnhilde on horse towards of Africa/ Courtyard door.
23:55	They are through the door.
23:59	Lift ring down and roll it into America.
00:00	Set the ring rolling and step into wings.

00:01   Have a rest, have a beer and meet your fans.

Kay Wilton: Costume Making

20:00   Asia - start making Brünnhilde's immolation costume.

23:26   Dress Brünnhilde in the costume you have made. Then leave.

Graeme Rose: Siegfried

19:57   Enter from Australia door. Walk across to Africa.
20:03   Enter Africa. Walk across Africa to America.

20:06   Turn around and enter America backwards, walk half way across the space backwards then turn and still walking backwards approach Position A. When close to Position A turn, start waving and continue to approach Position A (we are playing this scene in reverse and you are leaving not arriving).

20:10   Arrive at Position A. Kiss Brünnhilde farewell (try not to stand on her costume).

20:11   Slowly bring your arms up as if delighted by a gift. Look at door to Courtyard (out of the corner of your eye try and spot when Brünnhilde, moves her arm back from gesturing at the going and synchronise your looking away from the door with this.

20:12   Clasp Brünnhilde's hands in yours kiss them, open them, take her ring off and with a flourish put it in your pocket.

20:13	Embrace Brünnhilde, extend your arms for the embrace as she retreats.
20:14	Stand, wave Hello just before she turns away from you.
20:15	Stand
20:16	Walk to America Courtyard door (action now forward). Discreetly give the ring to the person there. Climb onto the bicycle.
20:17	Start peddling gently.
20:39	When you stop in Africa stop peddling, get off it and face other actors.
20:40	Gesture hello to everyone (don't shake hands).
20:41	Hand out to get drink from goblet when it is offered.
20:43	Drink from goblet.
20:44	Look quizzically at your empty ring finger.
20:45	Look at Gutrune.
20:46	As she starts to hold her hand out to you take it and kiss it.
20:47	Let go of her hand.
20:48	Watch Hagen cut Gunther's hand.
20:49	Hold out your hand for Hagen to cut it.
20:50	Hold out your hand to shake Gunther's hand.
20:51	Shake hands with Gunther.
20:52	Holding his hand move towards the boat.
20:53	Get on the boat and let go of Gunther's hand.
20:54	Wave Goodbye then start paddling.
20:57	Boat should be in Asia, get off it and go to Speaking Clock table.
20:59 – 21:20	You are the Speaking Clock.
21:21	Rest on Sofa #2
21:26	Stand up. Put your hood up and start walking towards Africa.
21:31	Enter Africa, stand a few steps inside the door looking at orange flames.
21:33	Approach the flames and stand on them
21:35	Reach out for Brünnhilde's left wrist and hold it.
21:36	Reach out towards her hand with your other hand

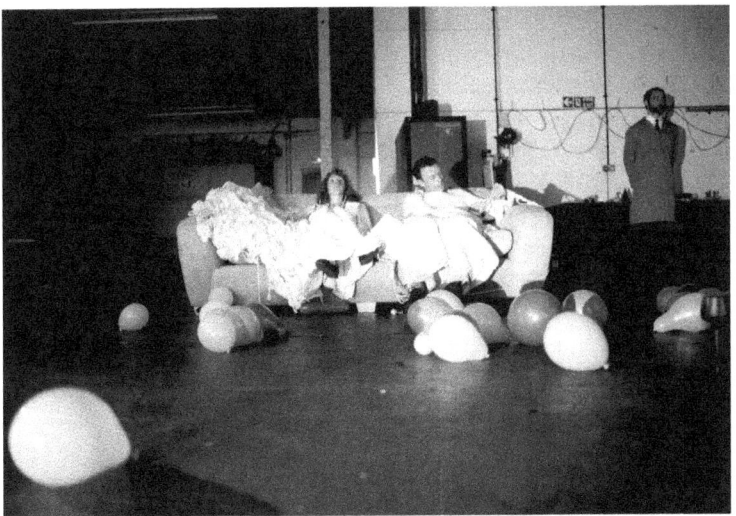

21:37	Take the ring off her finger.
21:38	Hold the ring up.
21:39	Back away.
21:41	Turn to leave and leave.
21:42	In Africa take off hood and go to rest on Sofa #2
21:54	Stand up and start walking towards Africa.
21:56	Enter Africa and walk towards people in room.
21:57	Stand facing group, you are telling the story of your adventure, indicate your hood.
21:58	Hold up the ring.
21:59	Kiss Gutrune's hand.
22:00	Hold Gutrune's hand and watch action.
22:12	You are delighted to see Brünnhilde and Gunther back.
22:13	Gesture (it's good to have you back)
22:14	Look concerned when Brünnhilde starts to shake.
22:15	Hold Gutrune's hand tighter (we are married).
22:16	Shake your head.
22:17	Look at Brünnhilde.
22:19	Hold up your hand with the ring on it.
22:21	Still with hand up look at Brünnhilde.
22:23	As people look at you, look round the group.
22:24	Shake your head whilst looking round the group.

22:25	Look at the spear.
22:26	Swear on the spear with your free hand.
22:27	Back away with Gutrune towards Asia.
22:30	Into Asia. Quickly change into wedding costume, brush your hair and drink beer.
22:33	Walk slowly into Africa along wedding path (dining roll) with Gutrune on your right arm.
22:37	Climb onto the bouncy castle. Try and have the ring put on your finger without any other contact. Try and kiss your wife without holding her. Then drink wine, eat sandwiches, sit in inflatable chairs.
22:46	Step off bouncy castle and move downstage to USL of the big ring and wait.
22:51	Hold the ring with your left hand.

22:52	Flirt with Rhinemaidens.
22:56	Argue with Rhinemaidens (you're not giving them the ring).
23:00	Wave Rhine Maidens off.
23:03	Turn to America.
23:04	Embrace new arrivals.
23:05	Tell a story of your hunting adventure (in slow motion).

23:07	Big laughs.
23:09	Drink potion.
23:10	Wait (something's happening).
23:11	You are remembering things about you, Brünnhilde and the ring.
23:13	You are distracted by passing umbrellas.
23:15	You are stabbed in the back.
23:16	Collapse onto the pallet.
23:19	Sit up a bit and tell everyone about your life.
23:24	Collapse and lie still on the pallet until the end of the show.
00:01	Have a rest, have a beer and meet your fans.

Instructions for the Speaking Clock.

Script: every minute you should say, "It is now [Time] precisely" Try and time your announcements so "precisely" falls at the instant the second hand points to 12.

For the time use the format "Nine forty two"
For hours use the format "Ten o'clock"
NB if you have 00:00 to call, just say "It is now Midnight".

On Thursday the show clock will be set 45 minutes forward so it reads 00:00 at the end of the show. Follow this time not the 'real world' time.

Tone: your vocal tone should be neutral but engaged. Please do not watch the show whilst performing this task. Occasionally some performers will be required to do tasks whilst performing the speaking clock. They should ensure they are always back for the marking of the minute.

Finishing: if your replacement fails to arrive at the specified time please keep going until doing so interferes with your next instruction but put your hand up at the point you think you should have been replaced.

Making *Twilightofthefreakingods*

Whilst at university I became fascinated by stories about the work of experimental theatre maker Robert Wilson. We were shown a grainy old VHS recording of a two part *Arena* documentary including footage of his early shows and I found them utterly compelling. These very long, very slow shows, mostly without words, just unfolding evolving surreal stage images, looked like they'd been beamed in from another plant.

The frustrating thing about theatre is that VHS recordings of the shows don't cut it at all. I was desperate to see one of Wilson's shows live but I couldn't imagine how that might ever happen. So, in my desperation, the only possibility seemed to be staging a show of my own that might mock up some of Wilson's tropes. Maybe this would give me some clue as to what the real thing was like!

As students making shows at Lancaster University in the late 80s we were encouraged to flex our artistic muscles. The only real issue was finding a spare slot in our performance space, The Playroom and a gap in enough people's diaries to secure a cast. Competition for both commodities was tight but this formal constraint was a spur for creative thinking. This was to be an unusual show, so it called for unusual methods. If I could do away with the need for rehearsals I would only require a single night in The Playroom and a single night of everyone's time.

So rehearsals were replaced with instructions, these told actors where they needed to be on stage when and what they needed to be doing. A map of the stage helped actors with the 'where' and a speaking clock calling every minute from 19:45 (the conventional Playroom start time) through until the midnight finish, told them when. Like players in an orchestra each actor's script only set out their part. Unlike players in an orchestra each actor had no idea what other the other performers would be doing.

There were no words, just music. The costume call was for everyone to be in blue jeans and a white t-shirt. The evening was promoted as having a cabaret atmosphere with chairs, round tables and the audience able to chat and drink during the performance. As a curiosity the performance drew a respectable crowd and to my surprise people seemed to like it. The night had a very strange and compelling atmosphere and the actors enjoyed themselves.

Thirty five years later, Stan's Cafe had decided to return a large portion of its enormous factory venue to its landlords. We needed to stage a celebratory farewell performance. At our opening night party five years before I had, recklessly promised, in front of a room full of VIPs, that our farewell performance would be *Götterdämmerung*. So there was our challenge, how to stage this vast opera with next to no money? I recalled the success of my 'no rehearsal' strategy from university and so *Twilightofthefreakingods* was conceived.

Our approach was simple. We would do away with the original music and in so doing replace a large orchestra with our long time collaborator Nina West. We would do away with the libretto and expensive singers and replace them with the actions of our actors. In every other way we adhered very closely to the original opera. We cast our associates and people who'd performed at the venue with other companies over the years in all the opera's named roles (there was no need for a chorus). We took a stopwatch to George Solti's recording of the opera, timed when all the key events occurred and put these at exactly the same moment in our production, building the whole visual / physical score around them.

Our venue comprised three long thin workshops parallel to each other with connecting doors and opening up to a courtyard at one end. At the other end a fourth workshop run perpendicular to and looking down onto the other three. We chose to put our audience on a seating bank and around cabaret tables in this fourth space where they would have to chose which workshop to look into at which point in the performance; conceptually the three performance workshops were organised as staging Past, Present and Future events.

In a budget saving, nostalgic act of 'intertextuality' we recycled props from previous productions so effectively our only significant purchase was a large piece of white fabric. Fortunately our show *Good and True* had been staged on a revolve, the key component of which was a very large metal ring. We hired a bouncy castle to give us a sense of Valhalla. Associate Artist Denise Stanton donated her existing sculptural costumes for the Siegfried and Brünnhilde plus, conveniently, she had made three very large bobbins which we borrowed for the show's opening.

We were set to go. On the fist night the cast admitted to being lost and terrified much of the time, which gave the performance an amazingly intense atmosphere. The second performance was much more assured, which meant it was more slick but possibly not as good.

In order to pull off the show's visuals we added three performing stage hands to the cast. These Machinists, pass unacknowledged by the rest of the cast. Conceptually they represent the industrial future of the space waiting to take over when the art is finished. For a number of years my daughter had been lobbying for a part in a show. Now, aged 8, she had her chance, she got to perform in the prologue. Having access to forklift trucks was too good an opportunity to ignore so we arranged to have Siegfried's corpse removed on a pallet lifted by forklift truck.

We commissioned our friends at Reel Access to make a film of the performance. Our interest was not in getting a straight documentation but instead prompting a new work of art. Our suggestion was that they play with speeding the action up as time-lapse, instead they did the opposite. They recognised that slowing down already unnaturally slow action creates a compelling movement quality that the brain appears unable to resolve into anything it recognises. In addition Reel Access layered action from different spaces over each other for long passages, so it becomes very difficult to distinguish which elements of the image belong in the same reality as each other (see above and opposite). It is a truly extraordinary film but difficult to find screening opportunities for given its duration and 'art house' nature.

As for the stage version of *Twilightofthefreakingods*, it will never happen again but we continue to look for opportunities to use this aesthetic and its timetable approach again.

About the illustration and design

The illustrations for the covers of these books were undertaken by students at Birmingham City University as the final module of their first-year illustration course during the Spring/Summer of 2018. The images were developed using workshops using variations of the theatre-devising methods produced by Stan's Cafe but adapted and applied to the making of visual work. The resulting work was shown in the pop-up exhibition *The Something Of Somebody Something* at AE Harris in May 2018.

The design concept of the books was produced by final year Graphic Design student Aimee Chapman. These were then further developed for print in a collaborative process between Stan's Cafe and the University's Innovation Product Support Service (IPSS) and involved helping the company with selecting appropriate DTP software, undertaking training and selecting a suitable print on demand service.

Gareth Courage
Lecturer in Illustration
Birmingham City University

www.ingramcontent.com/pod-product-compliance
Lightning Source LLC
Chambersburg PA
CBHW071757080526
44588CB00013B/2274